Literary Sexts
Volume 2

a collection of short & sexy love poems

Edited by
Amanda Oaks & Caitlyn Siehl

WORDS DANCE PUBLISHING
WordsDance.com

1st Edition
ISBN-13: 978-0692359594
ISBN-10: 0692359591

Cover & Interior Design by Amanda Oaks
Edited & Proofread by Amanda Oaks + Caitlyn Siehl

Words Dance Publishing
WordsDance.com

LITERARY SEXTS

VOLUME 2

THIS IS FOR THE LEATHER
& THE LACE OF YOU—

YOUR FLUSHED CHEEKS
& WHAT SET THEM ABLAZE

*People will come from all over the world
to see the way we love.*

-

Amirae Garcia

Do me deep. Heart deep. Do me like bone ache, like strip mining. Take iron ore. Take crude oil. Take ammonites. I am fragile and unholy. Open. Ravage. Eat.

- TANAKA MHISHI

Red fish, you are a strange hang. Ridiculous without water, my fingers feel up your noon star. Just tongue the wind and clouds of me.

- APRIL MICHELLE BRATTEN

The waters are rising. We build a submarine from scrap metal and blown glass. The land is eaten by the sea. We love in the entrails of our metal beast rough and water-rocked, four limbed creature of the deep.

- TANAKA MHISHI

Let me draw you in — my body is good and clean in your animal light.

— APRIL MICHELLE BRATTEN

Our orthodoxy is a fistful of bedsheet, and me on my knees before your altar of flesh and salt.

— TANAKA MHISHI

We slip our clothes off, slide carefully through the yard's dripping body. Snow melts under warmth. Air licks legs. We are a fresh want.

— APRIL MICHELLE BRATTEN

We are Picassoed by sadness. Eyes slip, noses elongate. Grief makes anarchy of our colours. I am the blue of deep space and entropy. Love me back between the lines.

- TANAKA MHISHI

My hands won't honor my mind, move like wild horses in arriving shadow. They find your skin, somehow, pry away the morning to get inside.

- APRIL MICHELLE BRATTEN

I want you to take a deep drag from me. I want you to pull me apart like a wishbone and whisper my name like it'll save you.

- TAYLOR RHODES

And then there's the path we followed, the tree that helped me hold you while we kissed minutes at a time—so sure the earth would swallow us whole.

- ROBERT LEE BREWER

I see you looking at me like you did a double take. I see your neck splintering like a tree struck by lightning. Baby, I'm gonna show you how to touch the center of the earth.

- TAYLOR RHODES

I picked these flowers, folded origami to say I am not just a fling, a song you learn to sing and forget. I want you to crack a smile and hum me a while.

- ROBERT LEE BREWER

13

There are groaning pine trees outside of my house and I can hear them breathing. There are words inside of you that spilled out of my mouth and I can feel them fluttering in your chest, all shaky: "I love you, I love you, touch me."

- TAYLOR RHODES

I stumbled to your thighs—pink sunset hills of no man's land. Let me get lost. Let me bring you alive.

- ASHE VERNON

With all of these "oh gods" dripping out of my mouth, you'd never believe I'm an Atheist.

- TAYLOR RHODES

I want you graffitied in the color of my lipstick—tag every contour of your ribs with the words "GOD IS DEAD BUT HE STILL SAVED ME. HE WAS REBORN IN THE SOFTNESS OF YOUR SKIN."

- ASHE VERNON

Hipbones like hard candy. I will suck you dry. I will fuck you so sweet and so threadbare so you will never fuck me over again. Hands like hard candy. Sticky. Stuck to me. Don't hold my hand, let me crack my jaw on your butterscotch backbone.

- OLIVIA WOLFE

You crawled into the spaces I dream in. Months since our last kiss and I still fuck you in my sleep.

- ASHE VERNON

This poem is good for One Free Overly Imagistic Metaphor about How I Really Just Want You to Sit on my Face.

- OLIVIA WOLFE

I may or may not be thinking about the various ways I can trace your tattoos with the tip of my tongue.

- LEAH RAMILLANO

Crying Old Crow and peaches you start ripping out your teeth—I mash your morphemes with my mouth – Catch your careless in my molars – I touch your bottom lip and it comes away wet with Her name – I still cannot wash the rot of peaches off my fingertips.

-OLIVIA WOLFE

I want you to fuck so much forgiveness into me that I forget why we were fighting in the first place.

— LEAH RAMILLANO

Your YES! like a Christmas tree— cranberry and lit up – You unwrap Me – pretend to be happy— I can take it back—I plead – You kiss someone else on New Year's Eve – but We fuck under the blinking lights of those dead pine needles.

— OLIVIA WOLFE

I think that I still look for you on the tips of strangers' tongues like a word that I know the meaning of but can never remember how to spell.

— LEAH RAMILLANO

If you're dark inside, I'll open the windows, & we'll be golden drenched. Outside, the grass aches for the backs of your knees. I'll lay you down on honey colored. I'll tell you the sun peaks. I'll show you how.

- CLAIRE NELSON

Sunrise behind us, I pressed you down like wild red horses freed from the chariot.

- JOHN SWAIN

If you were here, I'd drive you to Sweetheart Circle. We'd eat fruit salad from a big bowl. Come here, tell me again about the time we kissed, how we tumbled through the October night.

- CLAIRE NELSON

Sundress raised to your waist against the shade tree. Arms stretched up, breasts, the book of you opens below my body.

- JOHN SWAIN

You, my dark pocket of spinning, my deep joy against the side of your carport; tonight under the fool moon I long for your brutal pull. I want to not-touch until our hearts explode.

- CLAIRE NELSON

Kneel back to me. I raise red hair to kiss your neck. My crossed hands hold your secrets like a divine lake dreaming of Shiva arms.

- JOHN SWAIN

In your eyes, an emerald, a muse. Will I dance alone in your heart? I move best inside your pounding. At lunch, you extend your arm; it is all I can do not to lick the soft white inner side of it.

— CLAIRE NELSON

Open your mouth, all wet green trees and lightning inside, touch yourself storm in an endless sky.

— JOHN SWAIN

You're at my house for water then we leave. I don't mind. I want the mattress in your dank warehouse of treasures, you're Ariel's Florida brother, the rattle of the train wrecking my body as we roll through the night.

— CLAIRE NELSON

Our bed is desert; we meet each other with sand-filled mouths and find 100 different places that are synonymous with "oasis".

- GABRIELLE LUND

The first time I saw you, I remembered you. Your presence was planetary, I was caught in your orbit. How long did we circle, dancing, before we realigned?

- TAMI ELLISON

I am becoming a bilingual: I understand the language of your hands as if it was my native tongue. You are my Tower of Babel.

- GABRIELLE LUND

My hips are restless again. My legs, rivers of fire, hungry for your hard - opening now, inviting. Your lips leave wet offerings at my unlocked gate.

- TAMI ELLISON

I watch you laugh with the sunlight spilling through your teeth; you throw your head back and suddenly I am covered in morning.

- GABRIELLE LUND

When time takes you, my Love, and gravity slackens your jaw - I'll grab handfuls of ash, hold my fists tight against my weary heart, and turn memories into diamonds.

- TAMI ELLISON

The warm lift of water and your arms, the hiss and pull of ragged breathing beneath a slivered moon, stifled against your neck. Your eyes.

- SOSSITY CHIRICUZIO

I crave your breath. Your eyes, firelight on velvety cave walls. Your smile, the sun through October leaves. You move like the heartbeat of a mountain.

- TAMI ELLISON

It is the ozone of you. The sea salt spray and crashing waves of you. The thunderous cloudbank of you, rolling over me. Pulling my tides.

- SOSSITY CHIRICUZIO

23

Some silences are drawn out like icicles after a whiteout of words leave us paralyzed. My shadow freezes to the wall, blossoms retract back into themselves, waiting for the sun of your mouth to blush my skin into forgiving it.

- AMANDA OAKS

I am baptized in your water eyes. My body is new again in the river of you.

- CAITLYN SIEHL

I will unzip your chest with my teeth & lie on the long of your softest rib bone to listen to the way your heart rallies your blood into unbuckling your belt without blinking— after, I will fall asleep to the purr of your backbone.

- AMANDA OAKS

I want to sleep in the arch of your back. Sing to it. My Bridge of Sighs. My Caracalla.

— CAITLYN SIEHL

I live inside the second before we kissed for the first time all day, lips barely brushing, breath against breath, hunger burning like a million linked stars pulsating, close to death, under my skin.

— AMANDA OAKS

Our soft bodies in my tiny bed. Our teeth tap dancing while your left leg dangles above the floor. Your clumsy mouth is my favorite place to laugh into.

— CAITLYN SIEHL

I want to drink you like expensive scotch, neat, in a room with a chandelier. Or maybe like cheap whiskey in the dim incandescent of a dirty watering hole, warm in my hand, burning on my lips.

- DANABELLE GUTIERREZ

You crash kisses into me like beer bottles on bar stools.

- SCHUYLER PECK

Let's order one last round and kiss in front of god and the rest of the drunks, then pour ourselves out into the night, following the moon anywhere but home.

- WILLIAM TAYLOR JR.

I want you, smelling like the earth, fresh out from the rain, running back to me clothes heavy and soaked with sky.

— SCHUYLER PECK

I watch your eyelids flutter with our fluidity, intertwining into a perfect rhythm that I could never hope to recreate in even my greatest love poem.

— KACIE BUCHKOSKI

Kiss me so loud the clothes are quiet when we peel off each other's shells. Love me with such volume the neighbors mistake our bodies for gunshots and we'll never run out of ammunition.

— SCHUYLER PECK

To hell with every barrier between us. I coax the blood swelled mosquito which fed on you, onto my naked body.

- ERIN WILSON

Your hands hummingbird along my hips, dip and drink. I know why they call this flower.

- CLAIR DUNLAP

Spring cracks open. Violets rend the soil. Insects hover. I wipe my brow and scratch my skin. The frenetic heat of the honey bee makes me anxious for a sweet sip.

- ERIN WILSON

Will you come and crack my spine, make a trough of my pelvis? Can I sing again to your wrists how beautifully they bend?

- CLAIR DUNLAP

The pomegranate suggests: is out there, on table, in bowl, that light touches contours, but nature lies. The pomegranate is: in here, moist with darkness, broken open. Is me. Is hive. You eat fruit's meat like a ravaged carnivore.

- ERIN WILSON

There are no fig leaves, no apples. Just an overripe peach waiting, your wide mouth with tongue catching rivers of golden summer light.

- CLAIR DUNLAP

Desire is fundamental, the lexicon of planets and moons, a sentence's structure, the lunar longing to pull you into me with the unequivocal dark power, like the black noun longs to pull the red verb inside it.

- ERIN WILSON

You are a mountain beside me. I am the slowest river. We are aglow.

- CLAIR DUNLAP

Your name like a caramel thing, burnt-sweet and sticky. In my mouth, dissolving, sugar cube, cherry-red, lips locked.

- J. JULIO LAURETA

I'm licking the salt of your body from my fingertips, never thought I'd find such a burning sea.

- CLAIR DUNLAP

I have been collecting your voice for ages - taking syllables here and there, burying them in memory like seeds. I forget where I leave them, only remembering when I hear you again, and then it's springtime, the first bloom, your hands soft on my skin.

- J. JULIO LAURETA

Here, we dip-dye our thighs, suck the sounds of opening, smile wet and weary.

- CLAIR DUNLAP

You, with your urge to fuck in a church— and me, with my want to mark your body with my bite. Some might find us monstrous.

- RACHEL NIX

Our debauchery electrifies my circuits in shudders of elation. If I were a lantern I would light the darkest depths of your chambers.

- CONSTANT WILLIAMS

Let us ask forgiveness for our sins after we've finished— or shall we just shout God's name in something like praise?

- RACHEL NIX

These mountains of yours have taken more lives than Everest. Inching closer to the top and I can hardly breathe. I bet you the world that I will barely make it out of here alive.

— CONSTANT WILLIAMS

The middle of an Alabama afternoon in late August is hot enough without my knees pressed into your vinyl seats as you are pressed into me.

— RACHEL NIX

Your body, a bolted cage; mine a feral beast. I know the ecstasy of a free life but I want forever to be trapped inside of you.

— CONSTANT WILLIAMS

Cities were sacked, entire civilizations raised and leveled, stars imploded and sucked up the crust of the universe when they heard those sultry words leave your lips.

- CONSTANT WILLIAMS

Do you remember the house? The one in the woods, where we hid from the beasts. Do you remember the love? Of course you do. And the lust. How with the wolves outside I howled, and like them I sank my teeth in flesh, as though the scars would mark you as mine forever.

- DANIELLA MICHALLEN

My back arched over the surface of the kitchen table, bent up, concave with one fixed kiss below. You leave whole notes around my wrists. I etch staves down your back, and the fermatas holding each beat in its curve.

- AMBER C BRODIE

Make me a paradox, wrap me in your rising contradiction. Tell me I'm beautiful with your hands around my throat, that I'm bad when you reach for my hand. Let's be filthy in silk, animals in a church, dark-alley saints. I'll be the scream in a whisper, and you the teeth in a kiss.

- DANIELLA MICHALLEN

You smell distantly of a slice of honeydew melon, and I want to be the one who grabs you underneath the chalky lights of this bar, show you the curves of you -- how I can eat you, until you are nothing but a rind.

- AMBER C BRODIE

Tonight my ridges are violent and gritty. If you're not willing to get a dirty love underneath your fingernails, pivot on your heel back downtown. I am not catharsis; I am a pair of crimson red lips, ready to bleed between yours.

- ALEXANDRA TERESÉ CRITSIMILIOS

Last night, I watched your hips touch his between flashes of light and beats. I want hands up and down me and your sweat in my ears.

- AMBER C BRODIE

My liberty is godless but tonight, your lips are holy. I am the restless disciple of your hands; I will be what they tell me to be. You are unhooking my faithless declaration with honeysuckle fingers, you're becoming my religion.

- ALEXANDRA TERESÉ CRITSIMILIOS

You're like a picture of Dali, melting my time, hunting long legged mammals across my canvas. Your smile is a timebomb, destroying my cellphone with dream cascades until the reeds get tangled up.

- ALEX DREPPEC

Call me Ariadne, and I'll thread you through every artery of my labyrinth heart. String a lyre from my second thoughts, Orpheus, and sing me out of every dark place I stumble into.

— S.T. GIBSON

Where you walk, shadows draw back and nothing escapes your light. Where you walk, gravity moves away from you and you divide the sea of people.

— ALEX DREPPEC

All this time I spent boarding my windows against you and you still stole in through the cracks, sifted over the furniture, and settled into the carpet, persistent as sand in a beach house.

— S.T. GIBSON

Leave lines, leave traces with your looks where we are blood corpuscles and eyes sing songs, where three rhythms live, two of them heartbeats, I'm waiting for you, then I have to follow.

- ALEX DREPPEC

I was the vagabond moon swallowed by your wandering star, the crescent sliver of light kissed into oblivion by your absolute eclipse.

- S.T. GIBSON

Kissing you didn't require practice. It was slipping back into my skin. It was our bodies adrift in dark water.

- LESLIE WISHNEVSKI

You, the one who spoke Spanish made English taste like marbles; taught my knees gravel and my tongue swallow.

- LINETTE REEMAN

It's 9:02pm, but the sound of your voice makes me feel like dawn. If we were close enough to touch, I'd be a morning person.

- LESLIE WISHNEVSKI

I pictured it like this: dirty dorm sheets, top bunk. You ripped a hole in my bra. We took our time. The only thing we know how to do with bodies that will never again be this young, this pale.

- MEGAN TOWNSEND

You sigh; dancing in the ash of separation. I shudder; the tragedy of years wasted. We collide; for the first time I make love with both eyes open.

- LESLIE WISHNEVSKI

I see something new each time I taste you. How do you so widen the hearth of my desire? I cannot hold my hunger for you.

- MEGAN TOWNSEND

We make love like near-death. You're a hell-bound man with heaven-streaked hands. I run towards the light.

- LESLIE WISHNEVSKI

My tongue will speak you into riverbed. Flood your throat until the drought of your heart becomes thirsty again.

- KARLA CORDERO

The way your heat covers me: gradually as your body rises over mine—sunrise apricity. Filling me, a tall glass; you, the choicest flushing wine.

- KRISTINA SHUE

The glasses are dirty with pinot noir lips and the candles run wax for you. I wait for our thighs to burn fire on the carpet where we once found god.

- KARLA CORDERO

I want to curl into your pocket like smoke. Hang over the ledge of your nipple and let your vascular drum beat all the world's worry from me.

- KRISTINA SHUE

Let me dribble peach juice down your chest. Let me trace a sugar road into your mouth, lick my fingers clean from your sin and drink your body whole.

- KARLA CORDERO

Love like a rat loves the dark. A termite loves the colony. Brain loves the body. I would let you take off my face to slide me into bed. Would kiss the soles of your feet, waiting to be trampled.

- KRISTINA SHUE

I never pretended to be anything less than what you see: a woman completely in love with you, the most dangerous kind of wolf. It was only when you buried your hands in my fur that I bit down.

— SARAEVE FERMIN

I want to curl into your navel like the hollow of an oak, drop into you with the tiniest ripple and cocoon in you, a holistic retreat to heal the gash of distance between our bodies.

— KRISTINA SHUE

Tired of names, let this only be colors: the red of your nail lacquer, matching the stem of your wine glass. Now, I brush my teeth while you sleep, your long hair everywhere. Later, I will braid it into my own, dream of you.

— SARAEVE FERMIN

Today, I ate an apple direct from a tree. Today, I thought of all the good things to put in my body. Today, I thought of you.

- KRISTINA SHUE

Like the most innocent love note, I have oragamied myself, eight year old clumsy but earnest, imagining our hearts counting stars on Maine shores. Close your eyes, hear the early morning lighthouse call. Find me in the salt spray. Water evaporates, come quickly love.

- SARAEVE FERMIN

Your hands might be small, but they feel like the entire Atlantic Ocean on my coastline skin.

- MARIA SANTONE

All these secret tunnels and roadmaps of veins and they all lead to a heart that beats like two shoes in the dryer when you walk past me.

- K WEBER

I want to hold you for so long that loving you becomes a muscle memory, so it's something I don't have to think about; but I will always be thinking about it.

- MARIA SANTONE

Against an autumn-bare tree, our bodies got distracted from such gifts as a grey-black moon only to enjoy skin. I howled. Leaf in my mouth.

- K WEBER

I am lace and I rip under your touch but that isn't the point; the point is that you touched me.

- MARIA SANTONE

We fuck like we're the only ones who do it right. You say my name and it comes out like a dark confession. Our mouths swing open like doors. Our mouths open and we spill into each other, like wine.

- TERA K.

My heart beats its way out of my chest when you so much as look at me; I don't know how I've survived fucking you so many times.

- MARIA SANTONE

We loved like a shipwreck. That is, with a pounding, a thrashing, a foaming kind of thunder, all desperate hunger. We lie strewn across each other like driftwood and my throat burns with your moist, your salt.

- TERA K.

Kiss me like the skyline kisses the sunset and I'll show you how many shades I can turn.

- MARIA SANTONE

I pretend to be untouchable but we're peeling each other back like orange rinds. I bloom in goosebumps. Your mouth tracks my skin like braille.

- TERA K.

You are an artist so you know exactly how to draw me out of myself and into you.

- MARIA SANTONE

Sometimes not even poetry can make me understand. You're not a flower or a star or a galaxy, you're an animal. I think that if I look away you'll bite until I bleed. I think that this is okay with me.

- KATELYN FREYDL

I love in a pitch that only you know how to listen for. Your touch is a melody that is always stuck in my head.

- MARIA SANTONE

String theory states that the universe sang itself into existence. We hum with that melody. This is the difference between dying and being fucked.

— KATELYN FREYDL

I am nothing but empty space, but you are always here to fill me.

— MARIA SANTONE

This is our baptism, the clammy fear between us like a crucifix. Your hands are my prayer beads. I don't go to church because I don't need to. There is something holy here.

— KATELYN FREYDL

I want to meet you in the crossroads of our legs and take you to the place where our padlock mouths can meet each other's chain link skin.

- MARIA SANTONE

I want to learn to paint so I can show the sky the wheatgrass growing across your jawline and the blushing arteries between your legs. I am falling for your centimeters.

- KEELY M. SHINNERS

Come close, let me splatter you with my primal perfume and taste your dripping chocolate skin. Our echoes arouse the sleeping meadow, ears perk from their night-beds. Sticky embraces smolder into dreaming.

- DEBORAH RAMOS

Paradise is this morning, with you. If heaven is this rotting fruit and dirty sheets, then darling, let me die.

- KEELY M. SHINNERS

Veiled in rumpled sheets, our dance drips down thrusting thighs and bites at my neck. Your hungry roots circle our ying-yang bodies, spilling ripe to feed the sweet center.

- DEBORAH RAMOS

Ancient men are still looking for the essence of God, but here I am, sugar cane on my lips, knowing that if there is meaning to hearts beating, it is in the confectionary of your hands.

- KEELY M. SHINNERS

51

I still search for you, leaning on the seawall, blowing smoke rings beneath the moon center. Maybe I just dreamed you, a fantasy of flesh and fluid, my breath frozen, afraid to break the spell.

- DEBORAH RAMOS

I imagine you taste ocean-infused — salty and sticky and rolling in to kiss the shore one thousand times before you're satisfied — like a glimpse from your home, your endless summer.

- KEELY M. SHINNERS

Sacred honey-ripe vulva drums you from the Elk-cave. Ancient golden smoke circles our naked altar. The canal fills, and my river becomes yours.

- DEBORAH RAMOS

AMIRAE GARCIA is a 21 year old college student from California. She believes in the power of words, beards, and lipstick.

TANAKA MHISHI is a writer, performance poet and mischief maker currently living in Brighton, UK. He blogs occasionally at tmhishi.tumblr.com. He likes thunderstorms and poems that try to save the world.

APRIL MICHELLE BRATTEN lives in North Dakota. She has had work appear in Southeast Review, Thrush Poetry Journal, and Grasslimb, among others. She is the editor of Up the Staircase Quarterly.

TAYLOR RHODES. Twenty. Published author. Wood nymph. Touches with purpose, kisses like she created sin. suckmycoccyx.tumblr.com

ROBERT LEE BREWER is the author of Solving the World's Problems (Press 53), which is kind of like literary sext e-mails. He does a lot of poetry-related stuff, so just follow him Twitter @robertleebrewer.

ASHE VERNON is a queer, feminist poet from Texas. She is in her last year of undergrad, majoring in theatre and looking to become a tattoo artist. More of her work can be found at latenightcornerstore.tumblr.com

OLIVIA WOLFE is originally from that beautiful part of Appalachia, Franklin, PA, or Pennsyl-tucky, as her father calls it. She is a student at the Indiana University of Pennsylvania, and when she isn't writing borderline angsty poetry, she studies Sociology with the hope of being a social worker upon graduation (We know—she's insane).

LEAH RAMILLANO is a freelance scenic designer and poet from Los Angeles, CA. She tends to wear her weirdness and heart on her sleeve; all are welcome to come take a look at both on her tumblr: leahmichelleramillano.tumblr.com

CLAIRE NELSON is a poet living in Savannah, Georgia specializing in sexts, clever status updates and Missed Connections. She received her MFA in Creative Writing from Florida State University.

JOHN SWAIN lives in Louisville, Kentucky. Red Paint Hill published his first collection, Ring the Sycamore Sky.

GABRIELLE LUND is currently a third year Writing Arts student at Rowan University with a passion for language; hoping to fill the world with more love poems than necessary. spokeninkwells.tumblr.com

TAMI ELLISON is a mom, nurse, and writer from Ohio. In her spare time, you can find her talking to rocks, chanting, and writing love letters to the universe.

SOSSITY CHIRICUZIO is a queer outlaw poet and writer, a working class sex radical storyteller. Protest chants, love notes, smut and hymn. What her friends parents often referred to as a bad influence, and possibly still do. Recent publications include: Adrienne Journal, Wilde Magazine, and The Outrider Review. More: sossitywrites.com.

AMANDA OAKS is the founding editor of Words Dance Publishing. She is the author of two poetry collections, Hurricane Mouth (NightBallet Press 2014) and I Eat Crow (Words Dance 2014). She is currently working on a collection of poems called, Raised on Pop Songs. She likes poems that bloody your mouth just to kiss it clean. amandaoaks.com.

CAITLYN SIEHL is a clueless poet from New Jersey who enjoys crying and talking to birds. She's in love with everything and it doesn't hurt. Not right now, anyway.

DANABELLE GUTIERREZ is a vagabond, born in the Philippines and raised everywhere, she has been moving from country to country and taking photographs along the way since she was eight-years old. Her three-decade long life journey seems to have taken a longer pit stop in Dubai where she now lives, loves, and writes. Danabelle is the author of I Long To Be The River. She is currently working on her second poetry book & Until The Dreams Come.

SCHUYLER PECK was born in the great upstate New York, and now studies under the wide Idaho skies. Writing has been her craft since she taught herself how to hold a pen, and these crooked pretty words have been coming out ever since. She hopes to reach people she might never meet, and wrap them in welcoming words. Websites: daisylongmile.com / schuylerpeck.tumblr.com

WILLIAM TAYLOR JR. lives and writes in the Tenderloin neighborhood of San Francisco. The Blood of a Tourist (Sunnyoutside, 2014) is his latest collection of poetry. He is a Pushcart Prize nominee and was a recipient of the 2013 Acker Award.

KACIE BUCHKOSKI is a student in Western Pennsylvania. She likes to write poems and read them.

ERIN WILSON lives in Northern Ontario, hellbent on touching the world intimately, and if a paradigm shift happens in the meantime, she won't complain. Well, if it is a positive shift, she won't. Her work has appeared recently at Up the Staircase Quarterly, Rust + Moth, The Blue Hour, and Poppy Road.

CLAIR DUNLAP grew up just outside of Seattle, where she started writing poems at the age of six. She currently resides in the Midwest and when she isn't writing, she can be found doing pilates or laughing. Her work has previously appeared in Words Dance, BLIND GLASS, and Germ Magazine.

J. JULIO LAURETA is a student at the Manhattan School of Music and an alumnus of the Interlochen Arts Academy, where he began his first forays into writing poetry. His work has been appeared in Winter Tangerine Review and Black Heart Magazine.

RACHEL NIX is a native of Northwest Alabama. Her work has been published in Spillway, The Summerset Review, and Bop Dead City. Rachel is the poetry editor at cahoodaloodaling; more of her poetry can be found at: chasingthegrey.com

CONSTANT WILLIAMS is a poet and freelance writer. He is from California but currently lives in the inspiring and eccentric city of Paris, France. He is working on his second anthology and publishing his first. To contact please email: constantwilliamspoetry@gmail.com

DANIELLA MICHALLEN was born in Sao Paulo, Brazil, although she claims her soul belongs Elsewhere— capital E. As real life bores her, she creates her own anyway she can: words, images, and daydreams featuring people and places that perhaps never existed.

AMBER C BRODIE is currently getting her MFA in Creative Writing and teaching at Fresno State University. Her poetry has been featured in Aquirelle, Glassworks, Canyon Voices, and Foothill Poetry. She spends her days in Fresno studying, drinking wine, and watching Food Network.

ALEXANDRA TERESÉ CRITSIMILIOS is currently a college student who enjoys drinking coffee, being close to the ocean, and Springtime in New York. She writes for catharsis, to know what hurts. Afraid her words may one day die with her, she has tentatively decided to share them with others. She really hopes you enjoy them.

ALEX DREPPEC born 1968 close to Frankfurt, German author with hundreds of publications in German journals and anthologies, both the most renowned and the best sold among them, and numerous publications in the US and the UK. "Wilhelm Busch" Prize 2004. www.dreppec.de/english_drep

S.T. GIBSON is a displaced Californian currently living in the mountains of North Carolina. She is a master of the odd compliment and the perfect cup of tea but is still working on getting the whole undergraduate thing down. Her work can be found in Literary Sexts Volume 1, Words Dance magazine, or online at sarahtaylorgibson.tumblr.com

LESLIE WISHNEVSKI, a Columbia College Chicago graduate, joined the ranks of faceless writers inhabiting Los Angeles. Her mental stability is credited to childlike faith and a supportive parents/sister combo in Kentucky. Her interests include: playing ukulele, binge-watching anime, creating odd nicknames for friends, bad jokes, and keeping up with web-comics. fromthecusp.tumblr.com

LINETTE REEMAN is a queer writer from the Jersey Shore and a freshman at Rowan University. She represented Loser Slam at the 2014 Individual World Poetry Slam and National Poetry Slam, and recently became Rowan's Grand Slam Champion. She is also a contributing writer for BITCHTOPIA Magazine and spends most of her free time looking up videos of birds.

MEGAN TOWNSEND is a first-year college student at Fordham University in the Bronx. She grew up in New York, and plans on double majoring in Theology and English to write about interfaith theology for the new generations.

KARLA CORDERO is currently an MFA candidate at San Diego State University. She is a contributing writer for Poetry International and cofounder and editor for SpitJournal, an online literary review for performance poetry. Her work is published or forthcoming in The NewerYork, Cleaver Magazine, The California Journal of Women Writers, Apeiron Review, and the Lucid Moose Lit Press: Gutter & Alleyways Anthology.

KRISTINA SHUE is a creative, a student, a writer, an observer, and a creator. You can learn more about her at kristinawritessometimes.tumblr.com

SARAEVE FERMIN is a performance poet and epilepsy advocate from New Jersey. She is the founding editor of Wicked Banshee Press (2014) and a 2013 Women of the World Poetry Slam Competitor. Her work is forthcoming or can be found in Transcendence, Ghost House Review and Red Paint Hill. : saraeve41.wix.com/saraevepoet

MARIA SANTONE currently attends Ohio University. She likes words and feminism and petting strangers' dogs on the street. She can be found at sweetestsecrets.tumblr.com.

K WEBER has her heart in Ohio and her home in Kentucky. Look for her November 2014 digital/audio collection of poems titled "i should have changed that stupid lock". Her website is at http://midwesternskirt.moonfruit.com and she is usually found in an uncomfortable desk chair.

TERA K. is an aspiring adult who lives in Dublin. She's still not entirely sure what she's doing here.

KATELYN FREYDL unfortunately resides in rural North Carolina. One day she hopes to live in Portland and become a real person.

KEELY M. SHINNERS is a writer and poet based in Claremont, California. Her work can be found in Insert Lit Mag Here and [in]visible Magazine. For more information, contact keelyshinners@gmail.com.

DEBORAH RAMOS grew up in Ocean Beach, California. Her poetry has appeared in publications such as SageWoman, Rattlesnake Press, Gypsy Daughter's Bagazine, A Year in Ink, and others. Deborah's collection, Road Warriors, was awarded the Best Unpublished Poetry Chapbook 2010, by the San Diego Book Awards Association. You can visit Deborah at aarmoryofaardvarks.com.

LITERARY SEXTS

A Collection of Short & Sexy Love Poems
(Volume 1)

| $12 | 42 pages | 5.5" x 8.5" | softcover |

ISBN: 978-0615959726

Literary Sexts is a modern day anthology of short love poems with subtle erotic undertones edited by Amanda Oaks & Caitlyn Siehl. Hovering around 50 contributors & 124 poems, this book reads is like one long & very intense conversation between two lovers. It's absolutely breathtaking. These are poems that you would text to your lover. Poems that you would slip into a back pocket, suitcase, wallet or purse on the sly. Poems that you would write on slips of paper & stick under your crush's windshield wiper. Poems that you would write on a Post-it note & leave on the bathroom mirror.

HIT #1
ON AMAZON'S
HOT NEW
RELEASE LIST!

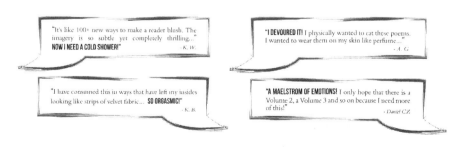

"It's like 100+ new ways to make a reader blush. The imagery is so subtle yet completely thrilling..." **NOW I NEED A COLD SHOWER!"**
- K. W.

"I DEVOURED IT! I physically wanted to eat these poems. I wanted to wear them on my skin like perfume..."
- A. G

"I have consumed this in ways that have left my insides looking like strips of velvet fabric... **SO ORGASMIC!"**
- K. B.

"A MAELSTROM OF EMOTIONS! I only hope that there is a Volume 2, a Volume 3 and so on because I need more of this!"
- Daniel C.Z.

POEM YOUR HEART OUT
Prompts, Poems & Room to Add Your Own
Volume 1

| $15 | 158 pages | 5.5" x 8.5" | softcover |

ISBN: 978-0692317464

PROMPT BOOK • ANTHOLOGY • WORKBOOK

Words Dance Publishing teamed up with the Writer's Digest's Poetic Asides blog to make their Poem-A-Day challenge this year even more spectacular!

Part poetry prompt book, part anthology of the best poems written during the 2014 April PAD(Poem-A-Day) Challenge on the Poetic Asides blog (by way of Writer's Digest) & part workbook, let both, the prompt & poem, inspire you to create your own poetic masterpieces. Maybe you participated in April & want to document your efforts during the month. Maybe you're starting now, like so many before you, with just a prompt, an example poem, & an invitation to poem your heart out! You're encouraged—heck, dared—to write your own poems inside of this book!

This book is sectioned off by Days, each section will hold the prompt for that day, the winning poem for that day & space for you to place the poem you wrote for that day's prompt inside.

Just a few of the guest judges: Amy King, Bob Hicok, Jericho Brown, Nate Pritts, Kristina Marie Darling & Nin Andrews...

Challenge yourself, your friend, a writing workshop or your class to this 30 Day Poem-A-Day Challenge!

THIS IS AN INVITATION TO POEM YOUR HEART OUT!

Other titles available from
WORDS DANCE PUBLISHING

I EAT CROW + BLUE COLLAR AT BEST
Poetry by Amanda Oaks + Zach Fishel

| $15 | 124 pages | 5.5" x 8.5" | softcover |

Home is where the heart is and both poets' hearts were raised in the Appalachian region of Western Pennsylvania surrounded by coal mines, sawmills, two-bit hotel taverns, farms, churches and cemeteries. These poems take that region by the throat and shake it until it's bloody and then, they breathe it back to life. This book is where you go when you're looking for nostalgia to kick you in the teeth. This is where you go when you're 200 miles away from a town you thought you'd never want to return to but suddenly you're pining for it.

Amanda and Zach grew up 30 miles from each other and met as adults through poetry. Explore both the male and female perspective of what it's like to grow up hemmed in by an area's economic struggle. These poems mine through life, love, longing and death, they're for home and away, and the inner strength that is not deterred by any of those things.

SPLIT BOOK #1

What are Split Books?

Two full-length books from two poets in one + there's a collaborative split between the poets in the middle!

COLLECT THEM ALL!

Other titles available from
WORDS DANCE PUBLISHING

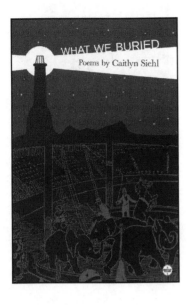

WHAT WE BURIED
Poetry by Caitlyn Siehl

| $12 | 64 pages | 5.5" x 8.5" | softcover |

ISBN: 978-0615985862

This book is a cemetery of truths buried alive. The light draws you in where you will find Caitlyn there digging. When you get close enough, she'll lean in & whisper, Baby, buried things will surface no matter what, get to them before they get to you first. Her unbounded love will propel you to pick up a shovel & help— even though the only thing you want to do is kiss her lips, kiss her hands, kiss every one of her stretch marks & the fire that is raging in pit of her stomach. She'll see your eyes made of devour & sadness, she'll hug you & say, Baby, if you eat me alive, I will cut my way out of your stomach. Don't let this be your funeral. Teach yourself to navigate the wound.

"It takes a true poet to write of love and desire in a way that manages to surprise and excite. Caitlyn Siehl does this in poem after poem and makes it seem effortless. Her work shines with a richness of language and basks in images that continue to delight and astound with multiple readings. What We Buried is a treasure from cover to cover."

— **WILLIAM TAYLOR JR.**
Author of *An Age of Monsters*

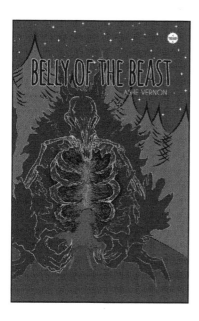

BELLY OF THE BEAST
Poetry by Ashe Vernon

| \$12 | 82 pages | 5.5" x 8.5" | softcover |
ISBN: 978-0692300541

"Into the Belly of the Beast we crawl with Ashe as our guide; into the dark visceral spaces where love, lust, descent and desire work their transformative magic and we find ourselves utterly altered in the reading. A truly gifted poet and truth-spiller, Ashe's metaphors create images within images, leading us to question the subjective truths, both shared and hidden, in personal relationship – to the other, and to oneself. Unflinching in her approach, her poetry gives voice to that which most struggle to admit – even if only to themselves. And as such, Belly of the Beast is a work of startling courage and rich depth – a darkly delicious pleasure."

— AMY PALKO
Goddess Guide, Digital Priestess & Writer

"It isn't often you find a book of poetry that is as unapologetic, as violent, as moving as this one. Ashe's writing is intense and visceral. You feel the punch in your gut while you're reading, but you don't question it. You know why it's there and you almost welcome it."

— CAITLYN SIEHL
Author of *What We Buried*

"The poems you are about to encounter are the fierce time capsules of girl-hood, girded with sharp elbows, surprise kisses, the meanders of wander-lust. We need voices this strong, this true for the singing reminds us that we are not alone, that someone, somewhere is listening for the faint pulse that is our wish to be seen. Grab hold, this voice will be with us forever."

— RA WASHINGTON
GuidetoKulchurCleveland.com

LOVE AND OTHER SMALL WARS

Poetry by Donna-Marie Riley

| $12 | 76 pages | 5.5" x 8.5" | softcover |

ISBN: 978-0615931111

Love and Other Small Wars reminds us that when you come back from combat usually the most fatal of wounds are not visible. Riley's debut collection is an arsenal of deeply personal poems that embody an intensity that is truly impressive yet their hands are tender. She enlists you. She gives you camouflage & a pair of boots so you can stay the course through the minefield of her heart. You will track the lovely flow of her soft yet fierce voice through a jungle of powerful imagery on womanhood, relationships, family, grief, sexuality & love, amidst other matters. Battles with the heart aren't easily won but Riley hits every mark. You'll be relieved that you're on the same side. Much like war, you'll come back from this book changed.

"Riley's work is wise, intense, affecting, and uniquely crafted. This collection illuminates her ability to write with both a gentle hand and a bold spirit. She inspires her readers and creates an indelible need inside of them to consume more of her exceptional poetry. I could read *Love and Other Small Wars* all day long…and I did."

— **APRIL MICHELLE BRATTEN**
editor of *Up the Staircase Quarterly*

"Riley's poems are personal, lyrical and so vibrant they practically leap off the page, which also makes them terrifying at times. A beautiful debut."

— **BIANCA STEWART**

SPARKLEFAT
Poetry by Melissa May

| $12 | 62 pages | 5.5" x 8.5" | softcover |

SparkleFat is a loud, unapologetic, intentional book of poetry about my body, about your body, about fat bodies and how they move through the world in every bit of their flash and spark and burst. Some of the poems are painful, some are raucous celebrations, some are reminders and love letters and quiet gifts back to the vessel that has traveled me so gracefully - some are a hymnal of yes, but all of them sparkle. All of them don't mind if you look – really. They built their own house of intention, and they draped that shit in lime green sequins. All of them intend to be seen. All of them have no more fucks to give about a world that wants them to be quiet.

"I didn't know how much I needed this book until I found myself, three pages in, ugly crying on the plane next to a concerned looking business man. This book is the most glorious, glittery pink permission slip. It made me want to go on a scavenger hunt for every speck of shame in my body and sing hot, sweaty R&B songs to it. There is no voice more authentic, generous and resounding than Melissa May. From her writing, to her performance, to her role in the community she delivers fierce integrity & staggering passion. From the first time I watched her nervously step to the mic, to the last time she crushed me in a slam, it is has been an honor to watch her astound the poetry slam world and inspire us all to be not just better writers but better people. We need her."

— **LAUREN ZUNIGA**
Author of *The Smell of Good Mud*

"*SparkleFat* is a firework display of un-shame. Melissa May's work celebrates all of the things we have been so long told deserved no streamers. This collection invites every fat body out to the dance and steams up the windows in the backseat of the car afterwards by kissing the spots we thought (or even hoped) no one noticed but are deserving of love just the same as our mouths."

— **RACHEL WILEY**
Author of the forthcoming *Fat Girl Finishing School*

Other titles available from
WORDS DANCE PUBLISHING

SHAKING THE TREES
Poetry by Azra Tabassum

| \$12 | 72 pages | 5.5" x 8.5" | softcover |

ISBN: 978-0692232408

From the very first page *Shaking the Trees* meets you at the edge of the forest, extends a limb & seduces you into taking a walk through the dark & light of connection. Suddenly, like a gunshot in the very-near distance, you find yourself traipsing though a full-blown love story that you can't find your way out of because the story is actually the landscape underneath your feet. It's okay though, you won't get lost– you won't go hungry. Azra shakes every tree along the way so their fruit blankets the ground before you. She picks up pieces & hands them to you but not before she shows you how she can love you so gently it will feel like she's unpeeling you carefully from yourself. She tells you that it isn't about the bite but the warm juice that slips from the lips down chin. She holds your hand when you're trudging through the messier parts, shoes getting stuck in the muck of it all, but you'll keep going with the pulp of the fruit still stuck in-between your teeth, the juice will dry in the crooks of your elbows & in the lines on your palms. You'll taste bittersweet for days.

"I honestly haven't read a collection like this before, or at least I can't remember having read one. My heart was wrecked by Azra. It's like that opening line in Fahrenheit 451 when Bradbury says, "It was a pleasure to burn." It really was a pleasure being wrecked by it."

— **NOURA**
of *NouraReads*

"I wanted to cry and cheer and fuck. I wanted to take the next person I saw and kiss them straight on the lips and say, "Remember this moment for the rest of your life."

— **CHELSEA MILLER**

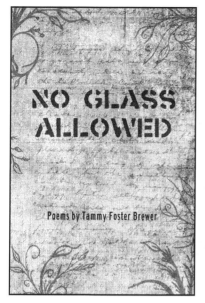

Tammy Foster Brewer is the type of poet who makes me wish I could write poetry instead of novels. From motherhood to love to work, Tammy's poems highlight the extraordinary in the ordinary and leave the reader wondering how he did not notice what was underneath all along. I first heard Tammy read 'The Problem is with Semantics' months ago, and it's stayed with me ever since. Now that I've read the entire collection, I only hope I can make room to keep every one of her poems in my heart and mind tomorrow and beyond.

— **NICOLE ROSS**, author

NO GLASS ALLOWED
Poetry by Tammy Foster Brewer

$12 | 56 pages | 6" x 9" | softcover | ISBN: 978-0615870007

Brewer's collection is filled with uncanny details that readers will wear like the accessories of womanhood. Fishing the Chattahoochee, sideways trees, pollen on a car, white dresses and breast milk, and so much more -- all parts of a deeply intellectual pondering of what is often painful and human regarding the other halves of mothers and daughters, husbands and wives, lovers and lost lovers, children and parents.

— **NICHOLAS BELARDES**
author of *Songs of the Glue Machines*

Tammy deftly juxtaposes distinct imagery with stories that seem to collide in her brilliant poetic mind. Stories of transmissions and trees and the words we utter, or don't. Of floods and forgiveness, conversations and car lanes, bread and beginnings, awe and expectations, desire and leaps of faith that leave one breathless, and renewed.

"When I say I am a poet / I mean my house has many windows" has to be one of the best descriptions of what it's like to be a contemporary female poet who not only holds down a day job and raises a family, but whose mind and heart regularly file away fleeting images and ideas that might later be woven into something permanent, and perhaps even beautiful. This ability is not easily acquired. It takes effort, and time, and the type of determination only some writers, like Tammy, possess and are willing to actively exercise.

— **KAREN DEGROOT CARTER**
author of *One Sister's Song*

a poem by kris ryan

Unrequited love? We've all been there.

Enter:

WHAT TO DO AFTER SHE SAYS NO
by Kris Ryan.

This skillfully designed 10-part poem explores what it's like to ache for someone. This is the book you buy yourself or a friend when you are going through a breakup or a one-sided crush, it's the perfect balance between aha, humor & heartbreak.

WHAT TO DO AFTER SHE SAYS NO
A Poem by Kris Ryan

$10 | 104 pages | 5" x 8" | softcover | ISBN: 978-0615870045

"*What to Do After She Says No* takes us from Shanghai to the interior of a refrigerator, but mostly dwells inside the injured human heart, exploring the aftermath of emotional betrayal. This poem is a compact blast of brutality, with such instructions as "Climb onto the roof and jump off. If you break your leg, you are awake. If you land without injury, pinch and twist at your arm until you wake up." Ryan's use of the imperative often leads us to a reality where pain is the only outcome, but this piece is not without tenderness, and certainly not without play, with sounds and images ricocheting off each other throughout. Anticipate the poetry you wish you knew about during your last bad breakup; this poem offers a first "foothold to climb out" from that universal experience."

— **LISA MANGINI**

"Reading Kris Ryan's *What To Do After She Says No* is like watching your heart pound outside of your chest. Both an unsettling visual experience and a hurricane of sadness and rebirth—this book demands more than just your attention, it takes a little bit of your soul, and in the end, makes everything feel whole again."

— **JOHN DORSEY**
author of *Tombstone Factory*

"*What to Do After She Says No* is exquisite. Truly, perfectly exquisite. It pulls you in on a familiar and wild ride of a heart blown open and a mind twisting in an effort to figure it all out. It's raw and vibrant...and in the same breath comforting. I want to crawl inside this book and live in a world where heartache is expressed so magnificently.

— **JO ANNA ROTHMAN**
MA, Coach & Conjurer of Electric Creative Wholeness

WORDS DANCE PUBLISHING has one aim:

To spread mind-blowing / heart-opening poetry.

Words Dance artfully & carefully wrangles words that were born to dance wildly in the heart-mind matrix. Rich, edgy, raw, emotionally-charged energy balled up & waiting to whip your eyes wild; we rally together words that were written to make your heart go boom right before they slay your mind. We like Poems that sneak up on you. Poems that make out with you. Poems that bloody your mouth just to kiss it clean. Poems that bite your cheek so you spend all day tonguing the wound. Poems that vandalize your heart. Poems that act like a tin can phone connecting you to your childhood. Fire Alarm Poems. Glitterbomb Poems. Jailbreak Poems. Poems that could marry the land or the sea; that are both the hero & the villain. Poems that are the matches when there is a city-wide power outage. Poems that throw you overboard just dive in & save your ass. Poems that push you down on the stoop in front of history's door screaming at you to knock. Poems that are soft enough to fall asleep on. Poems that will still be clinging to the walls inside of your bones on your 90th birthday. We like poems. Submit yours.

Words Dance Publishing is an independent press out of Pennsylvania. We work closely & collaboratively with all of our writers to ensure that their words continue to breathe in a sound & stunning home. Most importantly though, we leave the windows in these homes unlocked so you, the reader, can crawl in & throw one fuck of a house party.

To learn more about our books, authors, events & Words Dance Poetry Magazine, visit:

WORDSDANCE.COM